ISBN-13: 978-1508880127
ISBN-10: 1508880123

Character Creator

How to Create Believable Characters
Using the Myers-Briggs Type Indictor®

Cheryl Hindman

Table of Contents

Preface

My fascination with the Myers-Briggs Type Indicator® began as an undergraduate in college, when I learned that I am an INTJ (Introverted, iNtuitive, Thinking, Judging). At the time, I had no idea what it meant and didn't really care. I squirreled away the plethora of information I received about my type for another day.

As the years passed and I took on one miserable job after another, I revisited my INTJ profile only to realize that many of the jobs listed were in fact (and had been) aspirations and hobbies of mine. I felt foolish for not having given the questionnaire more weight in my younger years, and began to pursue a career more in line with my personality traits and collective style rather than financial need.

As one of my preferred MBTI® careers is that of a writer, I began to pursue the craft with more intensity. I tried my hand at poetry, greeting cards, short stories, and screenplays. I even wrote a few children's books after the birth of my twin boys, when I became a stay-at-home mom.

In watching my twins during the early years, I couldn't help but notice how different they were in terms of personality and interests. Although the MBTI questionnaire is not intended to be administered to young children, I determined their preferences by questioning them individually. I found that they were indeed complete opposites, specifically ISTJ (Introverted, Sensing, Thinking, Judging) and ENFP (Extraverted, iNtuitive, Feeling, Perceiving).

My ISTJ wants to be policemen, Mr. Law-and-Order, and indeed his type is one interested in security and maintaining the peace. My ENFP, on the other hand, is always creating, whether it be art, games, books, or costumes. Concentration is an issue for him, as it also is for his type. He is Mr. Possibility. Understanding their types enables me to point them in directions that may be of interest to them and alleviates struggles or conflicts between us where my personality may differ from theirs.

It's easy for me to say that my twins are complete opposites, but what does that really mean? How are they different? Where do their interests lie? How do these things affect how they relate to one another?

As a writer and creator of characters, I decided to create a portable yet cost-effective tool that writers can use to help add color and life to what may be otherwise be a one-dimensional character. The Character Creator can also help to create back story and determine relationships (or lack thereof).

If we writers try to stay "true to type," we can flesh out our characters and make them believable. I hope that you are able to benefit from this tool and that you have many years of prosperous writing in your future. Enjoy!

Why Type Matters

Why does a character's career matter? According to the 2013 American Time Use Survey from U.S. Bureau of Labor Statistics, employed persons between the ages 25 and 54, living in households with children under 18, spent "an average of 8.7 hours working or in work-related activities, 7.7 hours sleeping, 2.5 hours doing leisure and sports activities, and 1.3 hours caring for others, including children."*

During the "prime" of our lives, we spend more time working and in work-related activities than we do sleeping. Of course our career matters! If the wrong mattress can have an adverse effect on your sleep (and life), imagine what the wrong job could do? How can you create a believable character without taking their career, work life or working relationships into account?

Determining your character's career will determine more than just their income. How did they end up in that job? Was it by choice or circumstance? Are they content? Was it the job they wanted or studied to do? Who are their co-workers? Are they romantically involved with anyone at work or outside of work?

Personality types can greatly impact interpersonal relationships. Is your character romantically involved with anyone? If so, is their partner's personality type compatible with their own? How does this impact their relationship? What about familial relationships? Work relationships?

What if your character's personality type is incompatible with their significant other? Suppose they find somebody in their working life who is more compatible? How would this affect your story? What if your character met the wrong person at the right job, or the right person at the wrong job? How would this affect their choices moving forward? These

* Source: http://www.bls.gov/tus/charts

are just a few of the questions you can ask once you know your character's personality type.

When adding layers to your character, consider adding a hidden talent or hobby related to their personality type. Is it related to their career? If not, does it impact their behavior in a positive or negative fashion?

What about a character defect? Does your character lack confidence? Do they have emotional or physical scars (or both)? Do they suffer from addiction? Have these things prevented your character from getting the job they've always wanted? Did these things cause your character to lose their dream job? Giving your character imperfections makes them more believable.

Just as we refrain from stereotyping people in society, we must, as writers, refrain from stereotyping our characters. Keep in mind that genetics, environment, socio-economic status and education, among other factors, influence our behavior and our choices. All types are equal. Personality traits represent only one aspect of an individual. Be sure to take these other elements into consideration when layering your character.

Character Creator is designed to help writers flesh out and add layers to their characters to enhance their believability using the Myers-Briggs Type Indicator®. The MBTI® is one of the most widely used personality testing instruments in the world, generating sixteen specific personality types. At the heart of *Character Creator* is the idea that certain personality types tend to have an affinity for certain careers.

Character Creator contains templates for two dice, which, in combination, will yield one of the sixteen MBTI personality types. Each type has a corresponding card listing 20 different preferred professions for that specific type. (A template for a 20-sided die is also included.) The career listings in this text are far from exhaustive and represent a cross-sample of preferred careers from various sources.

If you come across a career path you've never heard of or know little about, be sure to check the U.S. Bureau of Labor Statistics, Office of Occupational Statistics and Employment Projections (http://www.bls.gov/ooh), which provides salary, educational and other data about different professions.

Additional resources are located at the end of this book. Because careers are an ever-evolving area, electronic sources and recently-published texts will provide the best data.

About the MBTI®

Based on concepts in Carl Jung's *Psychological Types* published in 1921, the Myers-Briggs Type Indicator® (MBTI®) was developed in the 1940s by the American mother-and-daughter team of Katherine C. Briggs and Isabel Briggs Myers. Distressed by the events of World War II, Myers wanted to create something that might help people better understand each other and avoid conflict.*

The initial questionnaire became the Myers–Briggs Type Indicator, first published in 1962. The MBTI is a questionnaire designed to measure psychological preferences in how people perceive the world and make decisions. Millions of people worldwide have since used this tool.

The MBTI measures an individual's preferences for four types of activity: Extraversion (E) or Introversion (I); Sensing (S) or iNtuition (N); Thinking (T) or Feeling (F); and Judging (J) or Perceiving (P). The various combinations of these preferences result in 16 different personality types.

The Extravert-Introvert scale indicates interaction preference and source of energy; the Sensing-iNtuition scale reveals world perception and method of receiving data; Thinking-Feeling indicates how conclusions are reached about data; and Judging-Perceiving indicates communication style and preference for dealing with the world. Each of the 16 personality types indicates a relatively predictable pattern of behavior.

Extraversion (E) vs. Introversion (I)

How do your characters derive their energy? From the world outside or from their inner world? Extraverts are energized by being with and around other people. They tend to be talkative, enthusiastic and animated. They learn and

*Source: http://mbtitoday.org/about-the-mbti-indicator/a-mini-history-of-the-myers-briggs-type-indicator/

9

work best through talking (they often talk more than listen), and are easier to get to know than Introverts. About three-quarters of the U.S. population is made up of Extraverts.

Introverts, on the other hand, re-energize by being alone. They prefer privacy, have fewer friends than Extraverts, and tend to avoid the limelight. Introverts are able to focus for long periods of time and are more inclined to listen than to speak. Only about a quarter of the population in the United States falls into this category.

Sensing (S) vs. Intuition (N)

How do your characters process information? Do they prefer concrete facts or would they rather leave things open to interpretation? Sensing individuals are direct and to the point and often focus on specific facts and details. They tend to work at a steady pace and value common sense. They tend to be more aware of their bodies and appearance than iNtuitives and prefer to master established skills.

iNtuitives are oriented toward the future. They value imagination and innovation, enjoy learning new things, and tend to focus on the big picture. iNtuitives like to work in bursts and often use figurative language, such as analogies and metaphors. They are more likely to have a graduate degree and are less concerned about their physical appearance.

Thinking (T) vs. Feeling (F)

How do your characters make decisions? Based on logic or based on people and circumstance? Thinkers are often found in strategic jobs and are good at cause and effect thinking. They naturally find flaws in others and can be critical at times. Thinkers are more assertive than Feelers and tend to get right to the point, preferring truth over tact. They are less sensitive to criticism than Feelers. In the U.S., Thinkers are more often male.

Tact for the Feeler is as important as truth. They prefer praise over criticism, are generally less assertive, and are more comfortable with small talk. Feelers are people pleasers and prefer to avoid conflict and confrontation. Very diplomatic in nature, Feelers are often found in professions dedicated to helping others. They are more sensitive to criticism from others than Thinkers. In the U.S., Feelers are more often female.

Judging (J) vs. Perceiving (P)

How do your characters structure their lives? Do they like to keep their options open or do they prefer finality? Judgers like structure, systems and organization in their life. They are driven to complete projects and prefer to work now and play later. They prefer jobs that offer control and can be very uncomfortable with change. Their work, living, and driving areas (cars) tend to be neat and tidy. Judgers represent about half of the U.S. population.

Perceivers prefer to keep their options open. They would rather play now and work later. Often spontaneous, Perceivers enjoy change and like jobs that are fun. They may start projects only to leave them unfinished. Time and deadlines are not important. Their work and living space (and cars) tend to be messy and cluttered. Perceivers represent the other half of the U.S. population.

By identifying interpersonal communication preferences, strengths and weaknesses, the MBTI may be used to improve work and personal relationships. The instrument is often used to build efficient teams in the workplace or to provide career counseling in academic environments. Just imagine what this information could do for your characters!

Assembling the Tools

Creating the Career Cards

Carefully remove pages 35 to 50 from *Character Creator.* If you wish to preserve the book for future reference, make double-sided copies of these pages (preferably on card stock). Cut the cards out and have them laminated to protect them during use (a cost-effective approach would be to use clear packing tape on both sides to laminate them). The dice will determine which card(s) to use when generating your character(s).

Creating the Dice

The dice are on pages 51 through 54. Cut the MBTI® dice out along the lines including the tabs. (Again, you may wish to copy these pages to keep the book intact.) Fold along all lines to form two four-sided dice. You may want to add a small amount of glue to the tabs prior to assembly to help the dice hold their shape. You can also cover the seams of the dice with a small amount of clear tape or cover the entire dice with clear packing tape after they are formed to help protect and maintain their shape.

When reading the dice, read the two-letter combination from the die with the star in the center first. This die will indicate the first two letters in the MBTI sequence.

In case you can't decide which of the 20 career paths to choose, use a 20-sided die. You may already have or wish to purchase a 20-sided die. If not, there is an additional template in this book. (It is of a larger scale than a typical 20-sided die to ease in assembly and reading.) Cut and form this die in the same fashion as the MBTI dice. Your *Character Creator* tools are ready to go! Take them with you wherever you write!

Using Character Creator

How do I use the *Character Creator?*

There are a few options for how and when to use the *Character Creator.* If you stumble upon a career or profession that is unfamiliar to you, just look it up online. You can also use the Bureau of Labor Statics web site (http://www.bls.gov/ooh), which provides information about career training, median pay, growth outlook and more.

Roll the Dice

Roll the two MBTI dice and pick a type (remember to read the starred die first). Let's say it lands on IN-TJ; locate the card marked INTJ and randomly select one of the twenty professions listed. If you can't decide on a profession, roll the 20-sided die and leave it up to chance. Repeat this process for however many characters you have.

Shuffle the Cards

Another method would be to shuffle the cards. Randomly select a card for each character, then select a career from each card. Again, you may use the 20-sided die to let chance decide for you.

Career-Driven Method

If you have knowledge of or wish to write about a specific industry, work backwards. Choose a selected profession from one of the cards (the same profession may appear on more than one card) and use the personality type associated with that career. Try selecting the same profession from two or more cards to yield two different personality types. How are these characters different? Do these differences cause problems between them?

Character Driven Method

Many famous people have their type listed in books or on the Internet. Are you basing your character on someone famous (past or present)? Use their type to select a card and determine a career. Then use aspects of their life to provide background and depth for your character.

Once you have a type, ask any or all of these questions:
- Are your characters working in their field?
- What training or education did they have?
- If they work together, what is their relationship?
- How are they similar? How are they different?
- Are their lives going the way they planned?
- If not, why not? How does this impact their behavior?
- Do their traits differ from what you had in mind?

When should I use the *Character Creator*?

You can use the *Character Creator* at any point in your story to add layers to your characters or to create fodder for turning points, backstory or conflicts between characters. You may wish to employ a specific story structure, such as Aristotle's three-act structure or Gustav Freytag's "Pyramid," among others.

Aristotelian Three Act Structure

Inherited from Greek philosopher Aristotle's *Poetics*, the three-act structure is a model that has been used throughout the centuries by writers worldwide. It divides the narrative into three parts: setup, conflict and resolution. The setup establishes the characters and their relationships and generally concludes with an event or turning point, known as the inciting incident.

The second act depicts the main character's attempt to resolve the problem introduced during the inciting incident. The character must change in some way, either by learning a new skill or by achieving a higher sense of self-awareness. This is referred to the character arc. The resolution consists of a climax or sequence in which the main tensions of the story are resolved, leaving the main character with a new sense of self.

Perhaps your character has the perfect job and then loses it. Perhaps they finally obtain a long-sought-after promotion. This could provide the inciting incident at the end of act one. Consider your character's type. Is this a positive or negative change? How will their type and the types of those around them drive your story?

Freytag's Pyramid

Another commonly-used story structure comes from German playwright and novelist Gustav Freytag, who wrote about the five-act dramatic structure in *Die Technik des Dramas*. What is known as "Freytag's Pyramid" consists of five parts: exposition (setting, backstory), rising action (series of events building to climax), climax, falling action (conflict between characters unravels), and dénouement (conclusion).

Perhaps your character is stuck in a dead-end job, which leads to depression, resentment, theft, or addiction. How can these events unfold and build to a climax? Can they be resolved? What are the personality types of those around your main character? At what point in Freytag's Pyramid do their types come into play?

Other Story Structures

Writer's Digest Magazine suggests four structures often used by writers: milieu, idea, character and event. To follow is a brief description of these structures.

Milieu Story Structure

This structure is most common in science fiction and fantasy. The milieu story begins when the character arrives and ends when the character leaves or decides not to leave (think Wizard of Oz). What happens before the character arrives is of little importance. If you are most concerned about having your character explore and discover the world you've created, use this structure.

The Idea Story Structure

The idea story begins by raising a question and ends when the question is answered (mysteries often use this structure). The story begins when something takes place (a crime) and ends when identity and motive are revealed.

The Character Story Structure

Character stories focus on the transformation of a character's role in an area that matters most. It begins at the moment when the main character becomes unhappy, impatient or angry and begins the process of change. It ends when the character settles into a new role or gives up the struggle (happily or not).

The Event Story Structure

In the event story, something is wrong with the universe (fantasy and science fiction often use this structure). The event story begins when the character whose actions matter most (to restoring order) becomes involved. The event story ends at the point when a new order is established, the old order is restored, or when order is destroyed. (Writers of event stories, skip the prologue!)

Whatever structure you decide to use, remember to always throw chaos at your characters. An uneventful story is not worth telling. Push your mind to the limits.

The Extraverts

ENFJ
(Extraverted, iNtuitive, Feeling, Judging)
*"The Givers"**

ENFJs find potential in everyone. Because they are highly attuned to the needs and motivations of others, they often excel in teaching and counseling roles (or any position requiring interaction). ENFJs enjoy learning new things and prefer an environment that offers a variety of projects and opportunities. Some preferred careers are:

1. Advertising Account Executive
2. Bilingual Education Teacher
3. College Professor (Humanities)
4. Customer Service Representative
5. Director, Child Care Center
6. Elder Care Specialist
7. Event Planner
8. Holistic Health Practitioner
9. Hotel / Restaurant Manager
10. Interpreter / Translator
11. Life Coach
12. Magazine Editor
13. Marketing Manager
14. Marriage / Family Therapist
15. Online Educator
16. Public Relations Specialist
17. Sales / Team Trainer
18. Set Designer
19. Substance Abuse Counselor
20. Urban / Regional Planner

* MBTI "portraits" courtesy of http://www.personalitypage.com.

ENFP

(Extraverted, iNtuitive, Feeling, Perceiving)
"The Inspirers"

Enthusiastic and imaginative, ENFPs enjoy challenging yet flexible work environments. They enjoy work that allows them to support the needs of others and see life as full of possibilities. ENFPs work best in supportive environments that recognize employee contributions. ENFPs are skilled at motivating others and excel in negotiating and counseling careers paths. Some preferred careers for the ENFP are:

1. Advertising Creative Director
2. Bilingual Education Teacher
3. Blogger / Writer
4. Cartoonist / Animator
5. Character Actor
6. Consultant
7. Dietician / Nutritionist
8. Holistic Health Practitioner
9. Inventor / Entrepreneur
10. Market Research Analyst
11. Massage Therapist
12. Newscaster
13. Occupational Therapist
14. Physical Therapist
15. Public Relations Specialist
16. Rehabilitation Counselor
17. Restaurateur
18. Social Media Manager
19. Speech Pathologist / Audiologist
20. Substance Abuse Counselor

ENTJ
(Extraverted, iNtuitive, Thinking, Judging)
"The Executives"

ENTJs are visionary and enjoy long-term planning. They easily spot system inefficiency and like to remedy or improve it. Sometimes forceful in presenting their ideas, ENTJs readily seek and share knowledge with others. They are ambitious and hardworking and prefer to work with other creative and ambitious people. They are highly skilled at persuading others and achieving results. Some preferred careers for the ENTJ are:

1. Advertising Account Manager
2. Biomedical / Chemical Engineer
3. College Professor (Science)
4. Computer Programmer
5. Cyber Security Consultant
6. Franchise Owner
7. Health Care Administrator
8. Human Resources Manager
9. Intellectual Property Attorney
10. International Banker
11. Market Research Analyst
12. Personal Financial Advisor
13. Pilot
14. Police Supervisor
15. Real Estate Manager
16. Robotics Network Manager
17. Sales Manager
18. Stockbroker
19. Surgeon
20. Venture Capitalist

ENTP

(Extraverted, iNtuitive, Thinking, Perceiving)
"The Visionaries"

Bored by routine, ENTPs seldom do the same thing twice. They enjoy work that involves creativity, intuition and logic. ENTPs are good at reading other people and are skilled negotiators. They can be entertaining speakers. Often entrepreneurial, they can be found in political, creative and technical fields where they are frequently in leadership roles. Some preferred careers include:

1. Advertising Creative Director
2. Athletic Coach / Scout
3. Ballistics Expert
4. Chiropractor
5. Detective
6. Diversity Manager / Trainer
7. Entrepreneur / Inventor
8. Management Consultant
9. Networking Specialist
10. Ombudsman
11. Outplacement Consultant
12. Personal Financial Advisor
13. Politician
14. Public Relations Specialist
15. Radio / TV Talk Show Host
16. Real Estate Developer
17. Reporter / Correspondent
18. Restaurant Owner
19. Social Media Manager
20. Urban Planner

ESFJ
(Extraverted, Sensing, Feeling, Judging)
"The Caregivers"

Warmhearted, conscientious, and cooperative, ESFJs seek harmony in their environment (and are determined to get it). ESFJs prefer to serve other people, often taking note of other's needs, and relish in the success of others. They want to be appreciated for who they are and for what they contribute. They prefer to work for employers who take care of their employees. Some preferred careers for ESFJs are:

1. Administrative Assistant
2. Athletic Coach
3. Bilingual Education
4. Child Welfare Counselor
5. Customer Service Manager
6. Dental Hygienist
7. Dietician / Nutritionist
8. Fitness Instructor
9. Flight Attendant
10. Home Health Aide
11. Interpreter / Translator
12. Medical / Dental Assistant
13. Minister / Priest / Rabbi
14. Paralegal / Legal Assistant
15. Physical Therapist
16. Radiation Therapist
17. Real Estate Appraiser
18. Registered Nurse
19. Social Worker
20. Veterinarian

ESFP

(Extraverted, Sensing, Feeling, Perceiving)
"The Performers"

Outgoing, friendly, and accepting, ESFPs love life, people, and material comforts. They enjoy making things happen. Flexible and spontaneous, ESFPs adapt readily to new people and environments. They are great with details and are able to read others with ease. ESFPs enjoy work environments that are active, fun, flexible, and that provide opportunities for helping people in practical ways. Some ESFP careers are:

1. Administrative Assistant
2. Carpenter
3. Child Welfare Counselor
4. Dental Assistant / Hygienist
5. Dog Trainer / Groomer
6. Elementary School Teacher
7. Emergency Room Worker
8. Film Producer
9. Fire Investigator
10. Fitness Instructor
11. Insurance Agent / Broker
12. Painter / Sculptor
13. Pharmacy Technician
14. Photographer
15. Public Relations Specialist
16. Special Events Coordinator
17. Transplant Coordinator
18. Waiter / Waitress
19. Wardrobe Specialist
20. Zoologist

ESTJ
(Extraverted, Sensing, Thinking, Judging)
"The Guardians"

Practical, realistic and decisive, ESTJs are quick to organize projects and people to get things done. They also expect others to be task oriented. ESTJs are logical and systemic in thought and can sometimes be forceful when implementing their ideas. They prefer routine over change. ESTJs dislike wasting time and strive for efficiency. Preferred careers for the ESTJ include:

1. Athletic Trainer
2. Auditor / Internal Auditor
3. Bill Collector
4. Building Inspector
5. Construction Worker
6. Cost Estimator
7. Database Administrator
8. EEG Technician
9. Electrical Engineer
10. Food / Drug Scientist
11. Funeral Director
12. Industrial Engineer
13. Insurance Sales Agent
14. Lawyer / Paralegal
15. Pharmacist
16. Physician
17. Real Estate Appraiser
18. Sales Representative
19. School Principal
20. Ship / Boat Captain

ESTP
(Extraverted, Sensing, Thinking, Perceiving)
"The Doers"

ESTPs tend to be spontaneous and enjoy being active and involved with others. They prefer action when problem solving, seeking immediate results. Theories and concepts bore them, though they tend to be logical thinkers. ESTPs are excellent observers, enabling them to read people and respond well to situations. Flexible in nature, ESTPs enjoy taking risks and prefer variety and a good challenge. Some preferred careers are:

1. Ambulance Driver
2. Bartender
3. Biomedical Engineer
4. Brick / Stonemason
5. Chef / Cook
6. Construction Worker
7. Firefighter
8. Fitness Instructor
9. General Contractor
10. Insurance Agent
11. Management Consultant
12. Mechanic
13. Paramedic / EMT
14. Personal Fitness Trainer
15. Pest Control Expert
16. Private Investigator
17. Robotics Engineer
18. Ship Carpenter
19. Sportscaster
20. Video Game Developer

The Introverts

INFJ
(Introverted, iNtuitive, Feeling, Judging)
"The Protectors"

INFJs desire to understand what motivates people. It is this insightfulness that helps them to develop potential in others. They are conscientious and committed to their values and are driven by their vision of things. They are very creative and like to work independently. Some of the INFJs preferred careers are:

1. Artist / Graphic Designer
2. College Professor
3. Corporate Trainer
4. Dietitian / Nutritionist
5. Elder Care Specialist
6. Genealogist
7. Health Care Administrator
8. Holistic Health Practitioner
9. Human Resources Manager
10. Interior / Set Designer
11. Interpreter / Translator
12. Literary Agent / Editor
13. Marriage Therapist
14. Novelist / Playwright
15. Occupational Therapist
16. Psychologist
17. Religious Worker / Clergy
18. Social Worker
19. Speech Pathologist
20. Substance Abuse Counselor

INFP

(Introverted, iNtuitive, Feeling, Perceiving)
"The Idealists"

INFPs are idealistic, yet loyal to their values and to those who are important to them. They are quick to see possibilities and enjoy work that involves connecting people to those possibilities. INFPs like to express themselves creatively and prefer autonomy in their work environment. They prefer mentoring relationships, as they enjoy working one-on-one with people. Some preferred careers include:

1. Architect
2. Artist / Graphic Designer
3. College Professor
4. Corporate / Team Trainer
5. Curator
6. Customer Relations Manager
7. Diversity Manager
8. Early Childhood Education Teacher
9. Film Editor
10. Interpreter / Translator
11. Journalist / Writer
12. Librarian
13. Mental Health Counselor
14. Missionary
15. Musician / Composer
16. Occupational Therapist
17. Philanthropic Consultant
18. Physical Therapist
19. Public Health Educator
20. Social Worker

INTJ
(Introverted, iNtuitive, Thinking, Judging)
"The Scientist"

INTJs have original minds and a strong drive to implement their ideas and goals. They are quick to see patterns and enjoy problem solving, generating new ideas, and developing solutions. Skeptical yet independent, INTJs have high standards for themselves and others. They favor intellectual challenges and tend to be very focused. They are highly-skilled strategic planners. Some preferred careers for the INTJ type are:

1. Architect
2. Astronomer
3. Attorney / Litigator
4. Biomedical Researcher
5. College Professor
6. Computer Software Engineer
7. Curriculum Designer
8. Cyber Security Specialist
9. Database Administrator
10. Editor / Art Director
11. International Banker
12. Inventor
13. Market Research Analyst
14. Mathematician
15. Neurologist
16. Pharmaceutical Research
17. Psychiatrist
18. Robotics Engineer
19. Surgeon
20. Writer / Editorial Writer

INTP

(Introverted, iNtuitive, Thinking, Perceiving)
"The Thinkers"

Quiet and contained, INTPs are interested more in ideas than social interaction. They are able to focus in depth to solve problems of interest. They are skeptical, sometimes critical, and always analytical. INTPs prefer to conceptualize rather than implement and follow through on things. They enjoy working independently with theories and ideas in a flexible environment. Some preferred careers are:

1. Agent
2. Biophysicist
3. College Professor
4. Computer Programmer
5. Economist
6. Geneticist
7. Historian
8. Interpreter / Translator
9. Lawyer
10. Market Research Analyst
11. Mathematician
12. Mobile Application Developer
13. Networking Specialist
14. Neurologist
15. Online Educator
16. Personal Financial Advisor
17. Pharmacist
18. Plastic Surgeon
19. Software Developer
20. Veterinarian

ISFJ
(Introverted, Sensing, Feeling, Judging)
"The Nurturers"

Thorough and accurate, ISFJs strive to create an orderly and harmonious environment at work and at home. They enjoy helping people and tend to remember specifics about those important to them. They have a strong work ethic and appreciate clear expectations. ISFJs are good at task completion and have good one-on-one listening skills. They excel where the ability to remember facts and details are important. Some preferred careers include:

1. Administrative Assistant
2. Athletic Trainer
3. Biochemist
4. Bookkeeper
5. Child Welfare Counselor
6. Dental Hygienist
7. Dialysis Technician
8. Elder Care Specialist
9. Family Physician
10. Occupational Therapist
11. Paralegal
12. Physical Therapist
13. Preschool / Elementary Teacher
14. Probation Officer
15. Real Estate Agent
16. Registered Nurse
17. Religious Educator
18. Social Worker
19. Tech Support Agent
20. Veterinarian

ISFP
(Introverted, Sensing, Feeling, Perceiving)
"The Artists"

ISFPs enjoy the present and what's going on around them. They like to have their own space and work at their own pace. Loyal and committed to helping others (especially those important to them), ISFPs dislike conflict and try not to force their opinions or values on others. ISFPs tend to work quietly behind the scenes and enjoy expressing themselves in creative ways. ISFPs are often action oriented and love the outdoors. Preferred careers include:

1. Beautician
2. Bicycle Designer / Repairer
3. Carpenter
4. Dental Hygienist
5. Elementary School Teacher
6. Fashion Designer
7. Firefighter
8. Geologist
9. Home Health Aid
10. Jeweler
11. Medical Assistant
12. Paralegal
13. Personal Fitness Trainer
14. Physical Therapist
15. Preschool Teacher
16. Social Worker
17. Substance Abuse Counselor
18. Surgeon
19. Veterinarian
20. Visiting Nurse

ISTJ
(Introverted, Sensing, Thinking, Judging)
"The Duty Fulfillers"

Quiet, serious and responsible, the ISTJ takes pleasure in making all aspects of life orderly and organized. The ISTJ dislikes interruptions and enjoys work that requires precision and attention to detail. They are task oriented, dependable and are able to concentrate for long periods of time. ISTJs tend to be quiet and reserved individuals interested in security and peaceful living. Some preferred ISTJ careers include:

1. Accountant / Auditor
2. Computer Programmer
3. Construction Manager
4. Coroner
5. Cost Estimator
6. Dental Hygienist
7. Executive Assistant
8. Fire Prevention Specialist
9. General Surgeon
10. IRS Agent
11. Lab Technologist
12. Mechanic
13. Orthodontist
14. Paralegal
15. Pharmacist
16. Primary Care Physician
17. Real Estate Appraiser
18. School Principal
19. Technical Writer
20. Veterinarian

ISTP

(Introverted, Sensing, Thinking, Perceiving)

"The Mechanics"

ISTPs enjoy troubleshooting and problem solving. They are good with and can remember large amounts of information. They enjoy working independently and prefer to work outside of the office. ISTPs are good with hands-on work and at skilled trades. They enjoy excitement and are drawn to risk taking and adventure. ISTPs like to have fun and take time to pursue their leisure activities and hobbies. Some preferred careers are:

1. Bicycle Repairer
2. Brick Master
3. Carpenter
4. Civil Engineer
5. Commercial Artist
6. Computer Repairer
7. Construction Worker
8. Corrections Officer
9. Emergency Room Physician
10. Firefighter
11. Flight Instructor
12. Gunsmith
13. Landscape Architect
14. Mechanic
15. Networking Specialist
16. Organic Farmer
17. Private Investigator
18. Race Car Driver
19. Securities Analyst
20. Taxidermist

The Tools

ENFJ

1. Advertising Acct. Executive
2. Bilingual Education Teacher
3. College Professor
4. Customer Service Rep.
5. Director, Child Care Center
6. Elder Care Specialist
7. Event Planner
8. Holistic Health Practitioner
9. Hotel/Restaurant Manager
10. Interpreter/Translator
11. Life Coach
12. Magazine Editor
13. Marketing Manager
14. Marriage/Family Therapist
15. Online Educator
16. Public Relations Specialist
17. Sales/Team Trainer
18. Set Designer
19. Substance Abuse Counselor
20. Urban/Regional Planner

ENFP

1. Advertising Creative Director
2. Bilingual Education Teacher
3. Blogger/Writer
4. Cartoonist/Animator
5. Character Actor
6. Consultant
7. Dietician/Nutritionist
8. Holistic Health Practitioner
9. Inventor/Entrepreneur
10. Market Research Analyst
11. Massage Therapist
12. Newscaster
13. Occupational Therapist
14. Physical Therapist
15. Public Relations Specialist
16. Rehabilitation Counselor
17. Restaurateur
18. Social Media Manager
19. Speech Pathologist/Audiologist
20. Substance Abuse Counselor

CharacterCreator:INTJ~CharacterCreator:ESFP~CharacterCreator:ENTJ~CharacterCreator:ISTP~CharacterCreator:ENFJ~CharacterCreator:ISTJ~CharacterCreator:ESFJ~CharacterCreator:ESTJ~CharacterCreator:ISFJ~CharacterCreator:ESTP~CharacterCreator:ISFP~CharacterCreator:ENTP~**CharacterCreator**~CharacterCreator:INTP~CharacterCreator:INFJ~CharacterCreator:ENFP~CharacterCreator:INFP

CharacterCreator:INTJ~CharacterCreator:ESFP~CharacterCreator:ENTJ~CharacterCreator:ISTP~CharacterCreator:ENFJ~CharacterCreator:ISTJ~CharacterCreator:ESFJ~CharacterCreator:ESTJ~CharacterCreator:ISFJ~CharacterCreator:ESTP~CharacterCreator:ISFP~CharacterCreator:ENTP~**CharacterCreator**~CharacterCreator:INTP~CharacterCreator:INFJ~CharacterCreator:ENFP~CharacterCreator:INFP

CharacterCreator:INTJ~CharacterCreator:ESFP~CharacterCreator:ENTJ~CharacterCreator:ISTP~CharacterCreator:ENFJ~CharacterCreator:ISTJ~CharacterCreator:ESFJ~CharacterCreator:ESTJ~CharacterCreator:ISFJ~CharacterCreator:ESTP~CharacterCreator:ISFP~CharacterCreator:ENTP~**CharacterCreator**~CharacterCreator:INTP~CharacterCreator:INFJ~CharacterCreator:ENFP~CharacterCreator:INFP

CharacterCreator:INTJ~CharacterCreator:ESFP~CharacterCreator:ENTJ~CharacterCreator:ISTP~CharacterCreator:ENFJ~CharacterCreator:ISTJ~CharacterCreator:ESFJ~CharacterCreator:ESTJ~Character

ENTJ

1. Advertising Acct Manager
2. Biomedical/Chemical Engineer
3. College Professor (Science)
4. Computer Programmer
5. Cyber Security Consultant
6. Franchise Owner
7. Health Care Administrator
8. Human Resources Manager
9. Intellectual Property Attorney
10. International Banker
11. Market Research Analyst
12. Personal Financial Advisor
13. Pilot
14. Police Supervisor
15. Real Estate Manager
16. Robotics Network Manager
17. Sales Manager
18. Stockbroker
19. Surgeon
20. Venture Capitalist

ENTP

1. Advertising Creative Director
2. Athletic Coach/Scout
3. Ballistics Expert
4. Chiropractor
5. Detective
6. Diversity Manager/Trainer
7. Entrepreneur/Inventor
8. Management Consultant
9. Networking Specialist
10. Ombudsman
11. Outplacement Consultant
12. Personal Financial Advisor
13. Politician
14. Public Relations Specialist
15. Radio/TV Talk Show Host
16. Real Estate Developer
17. Reporter/Correspondent
18. Restaurant Owner
19. Social Media Manager
20. Urban Planner

CharacterCreator:INTJ~CharacterCreator:ESFP~CharacterCreator:ENTJ~CharacterCreator:ISTP~CharacterCreator:ENFJ~Character-Creator:ISTJ~CharacterCreator:ESFJ~CharacterCreator:ESTJ~CharacterCreator:ISFJ~CharacterCreator:ESTP~CharacterCreator:ISFP~CharacterCreator:ENTP~**CharacterCreator**~CharacterCreator:INTP~CharacterCreator:INFJ~CharacterCreator:ENFP~CharacterCreator:INFP CharacterCreator:INTJ~CharacterCreator:ESFP~CharacterCreator:ENTJ~CharacterCreator:ISTP~CharacterCreator:ENFJ~Character-Creator:ISTJ~CharacterCreator:ESFJ~CharacterCreator:ESTJ~CharacterCreator:ISFJ~CharacterCreator:ESTP~CharacterCreator:ISFP~CharacterCreator:ENTP~**CharacterCreator**~CharacterCreator:INTP~CharacterCreator:INFJ~CharacterCreator:ENFP~CharacterCreator:INFP CharacterCreator:INTJ~CharacterCreator:ESFP~CharacterCreator:ENTJ~CharacterCreator:ISTP~CharacterCreator:ENFJ~Character-Creator:ISTJ~CharacterCreator:ESFJ~CharacterCreator:ESTJ~CharacterCreator:ISFJ~CharacterCreator:ESTP~CharacterCreator:ISFP~CharacterCreator:ENTP~**CharacterCreator**~CharacterCreator:INTP~CharacterCreator:INFJ~CharacterCreator:ENFP~CharacterCreator:INFP CharacterCreator:INTJ~CharacterCreator:ESFP~CharacterCreator:ENTJ~CharacterCreator:ISTP~CharacterCreator:ENFJ~Character-Creator:ISTJ~CharacterCreator:ESFJ~CharacterCreator:ESTJ~Character

ESFJ

1. Administrative Assistant
2. Athletic Coach
3. Bilingual Education
4. Child Welfare Counselor
5. Customer Service Manager
6. Dental Hygienist
7. Dietician/Nutritionist
8. Fitness Instructor
9. Flight Attendant
10. Home Health Aide
11. Interpreter/Translator
12. Medical/Dental Assistant
13. Minister/Priest/Rabbi
14. Paralegal/Legal Assistant
15. Physical Therapist
16. Radiation Therapist
17. Real Estate Appraiser
18. Registered Nurse
19. Social Worker
20. Veterinarian

ESFP

1. Administrative Assistant
2. Carpenter
3. Child Welfare Counselor
4. Dental Assistant/Hygienist
5. Dog Trainer/Groomer
6. Elementary School Teacher
7. Emergency Room Worker
8. Film Producer
9. Fire Investigator
10. Fitness Instructor
11. Insurance Agent/Broker
12. Painter/Sculptor
13. Pharmacy Technician
14. Photographer
15. Public Relations Specialist
16. Special Events Coordinator
17. Transplant Coordinator
18. Waiter/Waitress
19. Wardrobe Specialist
20. Zoologist

CharacterCreator:INTJ~CharacterCreator:ESFP~CharacterCreator:ENTJ~CharacterCreator:ISTP~CharacterCreator:ENFJ~CharacterCreator:ISTJ~CharacterCreator:ESFJ~CharacterCreator:ESTJ~CharacterCreator:ISFJ~CharacterCreator:ESTP~CharacterCreator:ISFP~CharacterCreator:ENTP~**CharacterCreator**~CharacterCreator:INTP~CharacterCreator:INFJ~CharacterCreator:ENFP~CharacterCreator:INFP

CharacterCreator:INTJ~CharacterCreator:ESFP~CharacterCreator:ENTJ~CharacterCreator:ISTP~CharacterCreator:ENFJ~CharacterCreator:ISTJ~CharacterCreator:ESFJ~CharacterCreator:ESTJ~CharacterCreator:ISFJ~CharacterCreator:ESTP~CharacterCreator:ISFP~CharacterCreator:ENTP~**CharacterCreator**~CharacterCreator:INTP~CharacterCreator:INFJ~CharacterCreator:ENFP~CharacterCreator:INFP

CharacterCreator:INTJ~CharacterCreator:ESFP~CharacterCreator:ENTJ~CharacterCreator:ISTP~CharacterCreator:ENFJ~CharacterCreator:ISTJ~CharacterCreator:ESFJ~CharacterCreator:ESTJ~CharacterCreator:ISFJ~CharacterCreator:ESTP~CharacterCreator:ISFP~CharacterCreator:ENTP~**CharacterCreator**~CharacterCreator:INTP~CharacterCreator:INFJ~CharacterCreator:ENFP~CharacterCreator:INFP

CharacterCreator:INTJ~CharacterCreator:ESFP~CharacterCreator:ENTJ~CharacterCreator:ISTP~CharacterCreator:ENFJ~CharacterCreator:ISTJ~CharacterCreator:ESFJ~CharacterCreator:ESTJ~Character

ESTJ

1. Athletic Trainer	11. Funeral Director
2. Auditor/Internal Auditor	12. Industrial Engineer
3. Bill Collector	13. Insurance Sales Agent
4. Building Inspector	14. Lawyer/Paralegal
5. Construction Worker	15. Pharmacist
6. Cost Estimator	16. Physician
7. Database Administrator	17. Real Estate Appraiser
8. EEG Technician	18. Sales Representative
9. Electrical Engineer	19. School Principal
10. Food/Drug Scientist	20. Ship/Boat Captain

ESTP

1. Ambulance Driver	11. Management Consultant
2. Bartender	12. Mechanic
3. Biomedical Engineer	13. Paramedic/EMT
4. Brick/Stonemason	14. Personal Fitness Trainer
5. Chef/Cook	15. Pest Control Expert
6. Construction Worker	16. Private Investigator
7. Firefighter	17. Robotics Engineer
8. Fitness Instructor	18. Ship Carpenter
9. General Contractor	19. Sportscaster
10. Insurance Agent	20. Video Game Developer

CharacterCreator:INTJ~CharacterCreator:ESFP~CharacterCreator:ENTJ~CharacterCreator:ISTP~CharacterCreator:ENFJ~CharacterCreator:ISTJ~CharacterCreator:ESFJ~CharacterCreator:ESTJ~CharacterCreator:ISFJ~CharacterCreator:ESTP~CharacterCreator:ISFP~CharacterCreator:ENTP~**CharacterCreator**~CharacterCreator:INTP~CharacterCreator:INFJ~CharacterCreator:ENFP~CharacterCreator:INFP CharacterCreator:INTJ~CharacterCreator:ESFP~CharacterCreator:ENTJ~CharacterCreator:ISTP~CharacterCreator:ENFJ~CharacterCreator:ISTJ~CharacterCreator:ESFJ~CharacterCreator:ESTJ~CharacterCreator:ISFJ~CharacterCreator:ESTP~CharacterCreator:ISFP~CharacterCreator:ENTP~**CharacterCreator**~CharacterCreator:INTP~CharacterCreator:INFJ~CharacterCreator:ENFP~CharacterCreator:INFP CharacterCreator:INTJ~CharacterCreator:ESFP~CharacterCreator:ENTJ~CharacterCreator:ISTP~CharacterCreator:ENFJ~CharacterCreator:ISTJ~CharacterCreator:ESFJ~CharacterCreator:ESTJ~CharacterCreator:ISFJ~CharacterCreator:ESTP~CharacterCreator:ISFP~CharacterCreator:ENTP~**CharacterCreator**~CharacterCreator:INTP~CharacterCreator:INFJ~CharacterCreator:ENFP~CharacterCreator:INFP CharacterCreator:INTJ~CharacterCreator:ESFP~CharacterCreator:ENTJ~CharacterCreator:ISTP~CharacterCreator:ENFJ~CharacterCreator:ISTJ~CharacterCreator:ESFJ~CharacterCreator:ESTJ~Character

INFJ

1. Artist/Graphic Designer
2. College Professor
3. Corporate Trainer
4. Dietitian/Nutritionist
5. Elder Care Specialist
6. Genealogist
7. Health Care Administrator
8. Holistic Health Practitioner
9. Human Resources Manager
10. Interior/Set Designer
11. Interpreter/Translator
12. Literary Agent/Editor
13. Marriage Therapist
14. Novelist/Playwright
15. Occupational Therapist
16. Psychologist
17. Religious Worker/Clergy
18. Social Worker
19. Speech Pathologist
20. Substance Abuse Counselor

INFP

1. Architect
2. Artist/Graphic Designer
3. College Professor
4. Corporate/Team Trainer
5. Curator
6. Customer Relations Manager
7. Diversity Manager
8. Early Childhood Teacher
9. Film Editor
10. Interpreter/Translator
11. Journalist/Writer
12. Librarian
13. Mental Health Counselor
14. Missionary
15. Musician/Composer
16. Occupational Therapist
17. Philanthropic Consultant
18. Physical Therapist
19. Public Health Educator
20. Social Worker

*CharacterCreator:INTJ~CharacterCreator:ESFP~CharacterCreator:ENTJ~CharacterCreator:ISTP~CharacterCreator:ENFJ~CharacterCreator:ISTJ~CharacterCreator:ESFJ~CharacterCreator:ESTJ~CharacterCreator:ISFJ~CharacterCreator:ESTP~CharacterCreator:ISFP~CharacterCreator:ENTP~***CharacterCreator***~CharacterCreator:INTP~CharacterCreator:INFJ~CharacterCreator:ENFP~CharacterCreator:INFP CharacterCreator:INTJ~CharacterCreator:ESFP~CharacterCreator:ENTJ~CharacterCreator:ISTP~CharacterCreator:ENFJ~CharacterCreator:ISTJ~CharacterCreator:ESFJ~CharacterCreator:ESTJ~CharacterCreator:ISFJ~CharacterCreator:ESTP~CharacterCreator:ISFP~CharacterCreator:ENTP~***CharacterCreator***~CharacterCreator:INTP~CharacterCreator:INFJ~CharacterCreator:ENFP~CharacterCreator:INFP CharacterCreator:INTJ~CharacterCreator:ESFP~CharacterCreator:ENTJ~CharacterCreator:ISTP~CharacterCreator:ENFJ~CharacterCreator:ISTJ~CharacterCreator:ESFJ~CharacterCreator:ESTJ~CharacterCreator:ISFJ~CharacterCreator:ESTP~CharacterCreator:ISFP~CharacterCreator:ENTP~***CharacterCreator***~CharacterCreator:INTP~CharacterCreator:INFJ~CharacterCreator:ENFP~CharacterCreator:INFP CharacterCreator:INTJ~CharacterCreator:ESFP~CharacterCreator:ENTJ~CharacterCreator:ISTP~CharacterCreator:ENFJ~CharacterCreator:ISTJ~CharacterCreator:ESFJ~CharacterCreator:ESTJ~Character*

INTJ

1. Architect
2. Astronomer
3. Attorney/Litigator
4. Biomedical Researcher
5. College Professor
6. Computer Software Engineer
7. Curriculum Designer
8. Cyber Security Specialist
9. Database Administrator
10. Editor/Art Director
11. International Banker
12. Inventor
13. Market Research Analyst
14. Mathematician
15. Neurologist
16. Pharmaceutical Research
17. Psychiatrist
18. Robotics Engineer
19. Surgeon
20. Writer/Editorial Writer

INTP

1. Agent
2. Biophysicist
3. College Professor
4. Computer Programmer
5. Economist
6. Geneticist
7. Historian
8. Interpreter/Translator
9. Lawyer
10. Market Research Analyst
11. Mathematician
12. Mobile Application Developer
13. Networking Specialist
14. Neurologist
15. Online Educator
16. Personal Financial Advisor
17. Pharmacist
18. Plastic Surgeon
19. Software Developer
20. Veterinarian

*CharacterCreator:INTJ~CharacterCreator:ESFP~CharacterCreator:ENTJ~CharacterCreator:ISTP~CharacterCreator:ENFJ~CharacterCreator:ISTJ~CharacterCreator:ESFJ~CharacterCreator:ESTJ~CharacterCreator:ISFJ~CharacterCreator:ESTP~CharacterCreator:ISFP~CharacterCreator:ENTP~***CharacterCreator***~CharacterCreator:INTP~CharacterCreator:INFJ~CharacterCreator:ENFP~CharacterCreator:INFP*

*CharacterCreator:INTJ~CharacterCreator:ESFP~CharacterCreator:ENTJ~CharacterCreator:ISTP~CharacterCreator:ENFJ~CharacterCreator:ISTJ~CharacterCreator:ESFJ~CharacterCreator:ESTJ~CharacterCreator:ISFJ~CharacterCreator:ESTP~CharacterCreator:ISFP~CharacterCreator:ENTP~***CharacterCreator***~CharacterCreator:INTP~CharacterCreator:INFJ~CharacterCreator:ENFP~CharacterCreator:INFP*

*CharacterCreator:INTJ~CharacterCreator:ESFP~CharacterCreator:ENTJ~CharacterCreator:ISTP~CharacterCreator:ENFJ~CharacterCreator:ISTJ~CharacterCreator:ESFJ~CharacterCreator:ESTJ~CharacterCreator:ISFJ~CharacterCreator:ESTP~CharacterCreator:ISFP~CharacterCreator:ENTP~***CharacterCreator***~CharacterCreator:INTP~CharacterCreator:INFJ~CharacterCreator:ENFP~CharacterCreator:INFP*

CharacterCreator:INTJ~CharacterCreator:ESFP~CharacterCreator:ENTJ~CharacterCreator:ISTP~CharacterCreator:ENFJ~CharacterCreator:ISTJ~CharacterCreator:ESFJ~CharacterCreator:ESTJ~Character

ISFJ

1. Administrative Assistant
2. Athletic Trainer
3. Biochemist
4. Bookkeeper
5. Child Welfare Counselor
6. Dental Hygienist
7. Dialysis Technician
8. Elder Care Specialist
9. Family Physician
10. Occupational Therapist
11. Paralegal
12. Physical Therapist
13. Preschool/Elementary Teacher
14. Probation Officer
15. Real Estate Agent
16. Registered Nurse
17. Religious Educator
18. Social Worker
19. Tech Support Agent
20. Veterinarian

ISFP

1. Beautician
2. Bicycle Designer/Repairer
3. Carpenter
4. Dental Hygienist
5. Elementary School Teacher
6. Fashion Designer
7. Firefighter
8. Geologist
9. Home Health Aid
10. Jeweler
11. Medical Assistant
12. Paralegal
13. Personal Fitness Trainer
14. Physical Therapist
15. Preschool Teacher
16. Social Worker
17. Substance Abuse Counselor
18. Surgeon
19. Veterinarian
20. Visiting Nurse

*CharacterCreator:INTJ~CharacterCreator:ESFP~CharacterCreator:ENTJ~CharacterCreator:ISTP~CharacterCreator:ENFJ~CharacterCreator:ISTJ~CharacterCreator:ESFJ~CharacterCreator:ESTJ~CharacterCreator:ISFJ~CharacterCreator:ESTP~CharacterCreator:ISFP~CharacterCreator:ENTP~*CharacterCreator*~CharacterCreator:INTP~CharacterCreator:INFJ~CharacterCreator:ENFP~CharacterCreator:INFP*

*CharacterCreator:INTJ~CharacterCreator:ESFP~CharacterCreator:ENTJ~CharacterCreator:ISTP~CharacterCreator:ENFJ~CharacterCreator:ISTJ~CharacterCreator:ESFJ~CharacterCreator:ESTJ~CharacterCreator:ISFJ~CharacterCreator:ESTP~CharacterCreator:ISFP~CharacterCreator:ENTP~*CharacterCreator*~CharacterCreator:INTP~CharacterCreator:INFJ~CharacterCreator:ENFP~CharacterCreator:INFP*

*CharacterCreator:INTJ~CharacterCreator:ESFP~CharacterCreator:ENTJ~CharacterCreator:ISTP~CharacterCreator:ENFJ~CharacterCreator:ISTJ~CharacterCreator:ESFJ~CharacterCreator:ESTJ~CharacterCreator:ISFJ~CharacterCreator:ESTP~CharacterCreator:ISFP~CharacterCreator:ENTP~*CharacterCreator*~CharacterCreator:INTP~CharacterCreator:INFJ~CharacterCreator:ENFP~CharacterCreator:INFP*

CharacterCreator:INTJ~CharacterCreator:ESFP~CharacterCreator:ENTJ~CharacterCreator:ISTP~CharacterCreator:ENFJ~CharacterCreator:ISTJ~CharacterCreator:ESFJ~CharacterCreator:ESTJ~Character

ISTJ

1. Accountant/Auditor
2. Computer Programmer
3. Construction Manager
4. Coroner
5. Cost Estimator
6. Dental Hygienist
7. Executive Assistant
8. Fire Prevention Specialist
9. General Surgeon
10. IRS Agent
11. Lab Technologist
12. Mechanic
13. Orthodontist
14. Paralegal
15. Pharmacist
16. Primary Care Physician
17. Real Estate Appraiser
18. School Principal
19. Technical Writer
20. Veterinarian

ISTP

1. Bicycle Repairer
2. Brick Master
3. Carpenter
4. Civil Engineer
5. Commercial Artist
6. Computer Repairer
7. Construction Worker
8. Corrections Officer
9. Emergency Room Physician
10. Firefighter
11. Flight Instructor
12. Gunsmith
13. Landscape Architect
14. Mechanic
15. Networking Specialist
16. Organic Farmer
17. Private Investigator
18. Race Car Driver
19. Securities Analyst
20. Taxidermist

CharacterCreator:INTJ~CharacterCreator:ESFP~CharacterCreator:ENTJ~CharacterCreator:ISTP~CharacterCreator:ENFJ~CharacterCreator:ISTJ~CharacterCreator:ESFJ~CharacterCreator:ESTJ~CharacterCreator:ISFJ~CharacterCreator:ESTP~CharacterCreator:ISFP~CharacterCreator:ENTP~**CharacterCreator**~CharacterCreator:INTP~CharacterCreator:INFJ~CharacterCreator:ENFP~CharacterCreator:INFP
CharacterCreator:INTJ~CharacterCreator:ESFP~CharacterCreator:ENTJ~CharacterCreator:ISTP~CharacterCreator:ENFJ~CharacterCreator:ISTJ~CharacterCreator:ESFJ~CharacterCreator:ESTJ~CharacterCreator:ISFJ~CharacterCreator:ESTP~CharacterCreator:ISFP~CharacterCreator:ENTP~**CharacterCreator**~CharacterCreator:INTP~CharacterCreator:INFJ~CharacterCreator:ENFP~CharacterCreator:INFP
CharacterCreator:INTJ~CharacterCreator:ESFP~CharacterCreator:ENTJ~CharacterCreator:ISTP~CharacterCreator:ENFJ~CharacterCreator:ISTJ~CharacterCreator:ESFJ~CharacterCreator:ESTJ~CharacterCreator:ISFJ~CharacterCreator:ESTP~CharacterCreator:ISFP~CharacterCreator:ENTP~**CharacterCreator**~CharacterCreator:INTP~CharacterCreator:INFJ~CharacterCreator:ENFP~CharacterCreator:INFP
CharacterCreator:INTJ~CharacterCreator:ESFP~CharacterCreator:ENTJ~CharacterCreator:ISTP~CharacterCreator:ENFJ~CharacterCreator:ISTJ~CharacterCreator:ESFJ~CharacterCreator:ESTJ~CharacterCreator:Character

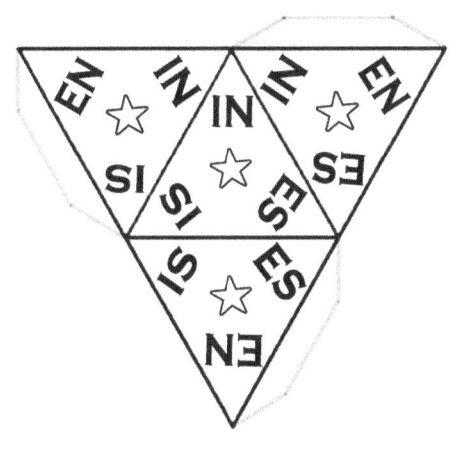

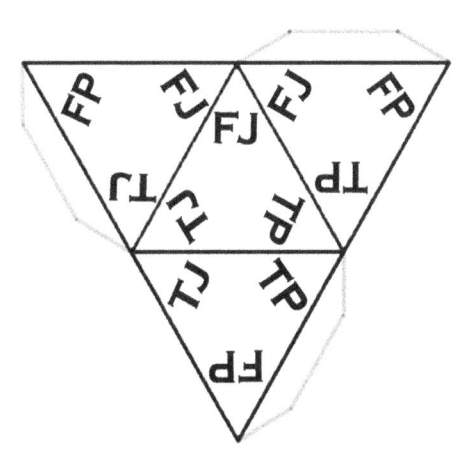

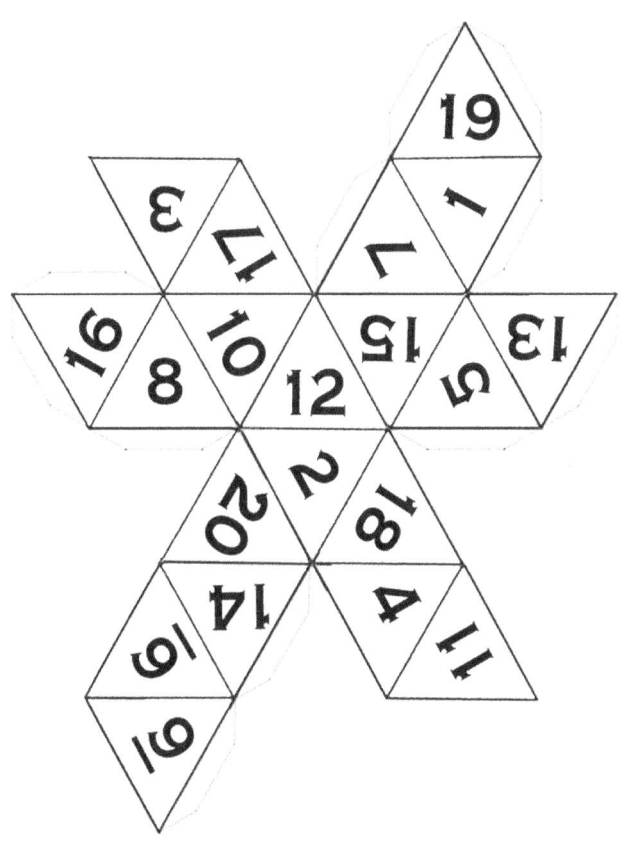

Suggested Reading

Feel free to explore the MBTI® and MBTI-related professions on your own, either from written or electronic sources. Some additional resources include:

Books and Printed Sources

Do What You Are: Discover the Perfect Career for You through the Secrets of Personality Type by Paul D. Tieger and Barbara Barron (2014).

Gifts Differing: Understanding Personality Type by Isabel Briggs Myers and Peter B. Myers (1995).

Electronic Resources

The Best Jobs for Every Personality Type by Richard Feloni and Skye Gould at http://www.businessinsider.com/best-jobs-for-every-personality-2014-9 (2014).

List of Personality Types and Matching Careers, by Michael T. Robinson. (http://www.careerplanner.com/List-of-Personality-Types-and-Careers.cfm).

MBTI® Basics, through the Myers and Briggs Foundation, (http://www.myersbriggs.org/my-mbti-personality-type/mbti-basics/).

U.S. Bureau of Labor Statistics, Office of Occupational Statistics and Employment Projections, (http://www.bls.gov/ooh).

www.ingramcontent.com/pod-product-compliance
Lightning Source LLC
Chambersburg PA
CBHW070622290526
45790CB00002B/953